THANKS
GW01606003

Ballantine Books • New York

MUCHO
APPRECIOSO!
JIM DAVIS

Ballantine Books • New York

Take my gratitude.
PLEASE!
JIM DAVIS

Ballantine Books • New York

THANKS... I NEEDED THAT

Ballantine Books • New York

TO: GIVER
FROM: GETTER
RE: THANKS
JIM DAVIS

Ballantine Books • New York

You did nice.
THANKS
JIM DAVIS

Ballantine Books • New York

You great.

Me grateful.

Ballantine Books • New York

Consider yourself appreciated
JIM DAVIS

Ballantine Books • New York

I AM
THANKING
YOO-OO-OO,
OO-OO-OO,
OO-OO, OO-
JIM DAVIS

Ballantine Books • New York

A note
of thanks
JIM DAVIS

Ballantine Books • New York

MY COMPLIMENTS TO THE CHEF

Ballantine Books • New York

THANKS.
G
JIM DAVIS

Ballantine Books • New York

I thank you.

My tummy thanks you.

Ballantine Books • New York

MANY THANKS
JIM DAVIS

Published under license from United Feature Syndicate, Inc., New York, NY and
by arrangement with Argus Communications, Allen, TX. Printed in U.S.A.

Ballantine Books • New York

I owe you one!

Ballantine Books • New York

Permit me to exude gratitude

Ballantine Books • New York

Thanks
a million.
Make that
2 million!
ONE DOLLAR
JIM DAVIS

Ballantine Books • New York

Thanks for the Hospitality
JIM DAVIS

Ballantine Books • New York

WORDS AREN'T ENOUGH.
MAY I KISS YOUR FEET?

Ballantine Books • New York

Your
thoughtfulness
is exceeded
only by my
gratefulness

Ballantine Books • New York

You're spoiling me.

Keep it up

Ballantine Books • New York

You're so thoughtful.

I'm so thankful.

Ballantine Books • New York

THANKS
NOW GET OUTA HERE
JIM DAVIS

Ballantine Books • New York

YOU GIVE GREAT GIFT!
JIM DAVIS

Ballantine Books • New York

I want to thank you...
and the members of the Academy
JIM DAVIS

Ballantine Books • New York

A GOOD TIME
WAS HAD
BY ALL
JIM DAVIS

Ballantine Books • New York

You
may
indulge
me
anytime

Ballantine Books • New York

For all
you do...
merci
beaucoup
JIM DAVIS

Ballantine Books • New York

DINNER WAS GREAT.
SAME TIME TOMORROW?
JIM DAVIS

Ballantine Books • New York

THANKS A BUNCH

Ballantine Books • New York